SPACEX

SPACEX

ODYSSEYS

CHRISTOPHER FOREST

CREATIVE EDUCATION · CREATIVE PAPERBACKS

Published by Creative Education and Creative Paperbacks
P.O. Box 227, Mankato, Minnesota 56002
Creative Education and Creative Paperbacks are imprints of
The Creative Company
www.thecreativecompany.us

Design by Blue Design
Art direction by Graham Morgan

Images by Getty Images/Aubrey Gemignani/NASA, 69, bgfoto, 44, dima_zel, 63, Handout, 38–39, Kevin Carter, 42, Mark Felix/Bloomberg, 59, Orlando Sentinel, 24, peepo, 51, SERGIO FLORES, 6; Unsplash/ANIRUDH, 37, Bill Jelen, 48, Jake Weirick, 75, NASA, 70–71, SpaceX, 2, 4–5, 16, 26, 47, Stephan Widua, 52, Sven Piper, 33; Wikimedia Commons/FlyingSinger, 12, NASA, 34–35, NASA/Joel Kowsky, 60, Patricia Moore, 64, SpaceX, cover, 11, 19, 30, Steve Jurvetson, 56, The Royal Society, 20, U.S. Army Kwajalein Atoll (USAKA), 8

Library of Congress Cataloging-in-Publication Data

Names: Forest, Christopher author
Title: SpaceX / by Christopher Forest.
Description: Mankato, Minnesota : Creative Education and Creative Paperbacks, [2026] | Series: Odysseys in business | Includes bibliographical references and index. | Audience: Ages 12-15 | Audience: Grades 7-9 | Summary: "Discover SpaceX's vision for space exploration, from reusable rockets to Mars missions. Inspire high-school age dreamers to explore how this company pushes the limits of human achievement. This title includes sidebars, a glossary, selected bibliography, websites, and an index"— Provided by publisher.
Identifiers: LCCN 2025021243 (print) | LCCN 2025021244 (ebook) | ISBN 9798895811375 library binding | ISBN 9798896800903 paperback | ISBN 9798895812631 ebook
Subjects: LCSH: SpaceX (Firm) | Launch vehicles (Astronautics) | Space flight—Juvenile literature | Space launch industry
Classification: LCC TL793 .F66 2026 (print) | LCC TL793 (ebook) | DDC 338.4/7629478—dc23/eng/20250725
LC record available at https://lccn.loc.gov/2025021243
LC ebook record available at https://lccn.loc.gov/2025021244

Printed in the United States

CONTENTS

Introduction

On September 28, 2008, all eyes were on the skies above the Ronald Reagan Ballistic Defense Test Site at the Kwajalein Atoll. This island region is an American military base 2,500 miles southwest of Hawaii in the in the Pacific Ocean. As the clock ticked to 7:15 PM (EDT), people nervously waited to see what might happen.

OPPOSITE: The Falcon 1 rocket was SpaceX's first orbital rocket, which paved the way for later designs.

Then, a Falcon 1 rocket launched from the base. People watched in anticipation as the craft ascended into the sky. Would the rocket actually make it into space, or would it explode before leaving the atmosphere?

A sigh of relief swept over everyone at SpaceX as the second stage of the Falcon 1 left the Earth's upper atmosphere and entered orbit. This achievement marked a historic moment for space travel—it was the first time a privately owned company launched a spacecraft into space. After three failed attempts to launch a similar Falcon 1, the company proved that a privately built rocket could successfully reach orbit.

"The fourth time's the charm," said SpaceX chairman Elon Musk. He was so proud of the successful launch that he declared it was "one of the best days of my life."

THE MARS SOCIETY
The 9th Annual
International Mars

In The Beginning

SpaceX was formed in 2002 by businessman and entrepreneur Elon Musk. Musk had already made a name for himself with his software company Zip2 and as co-founder of PayPal. He ultimately sold both for more than $1.8 billion and used that money to create Space Exploration Technologies Corporation, or SpaceX for short.

OPPOSITE: Elon Musk has always been fascinated with space and the idea of traveling to other planets.

Musk had created the company to improve space travel for humans. As NASA began developing plans to send humans to Mars, Musk thought he might be able to become a part of that plan. He hoped to develop a prototype greenhouse that could be used on the Red Planet. The greenhouse, called Mars Oasis, was part of a bigger vision Musk had to encourage people to explore Mars. He wanted to develop a future base and help establish a colony on the planet.

However, Musk soon discovered that his plans were quite costly. So, he changed the goal of SpaceX, hoping to capitalize on the rapidly changing nature of space travel. This shift came as a result of decisions made by the National Aeronautics and Space Administration (NASA). NASA is a United States government agency that coordinates American space travel. For years, the organization helped fund the development of spacecraft, manage missions to the moon, and coordinate space launches. It was the key American agency in the **space race** between the United States and the Soviet Union as well as central to the development of the space shuttle program.

owever, as costs skyrocketed and budgets were cut back, NASA changed its direction. It began looking for privately funded spacecraft to help carry humans, materials, and objects into space.

OPPOSITE SpaceX has prioritized reusable rockets as a core part of its mission to reduce spaceflight costs and make space more accessible.

Musk responded by reimagining SpaceX. He firmly believed that his company should strive to create spacecraft that could reliably fly more frequently into space. He believed this approach would result in more cost-effective space travel in a time when costs were growing. Musk also hoped that low-cost space travel would open space exploration to every human interested in visiting space.

However, making space travel cost effective was no easy task. Although Musk founded SpaceX in 2002, the development of the first rocket took years. This effort resulted in the creation of the Falcon 1, SpaceX's first type of rocket. These rockets were named after the Millennium Falcon, a spaceship from the Star Wars franchise.

During the first few years of development, Musk spent $100 million of his own money to get SpaceX off the ground. In addition to developing a rocket, the scientists at SpaceX also created a spacecraft called Dragon. The Dragon was the first SpaceX craft designed to transport people to and from space. Its unique name was inspired by the 1960s folk song "Puff the Magic Dragon," performed by Peter, Paul and Mary.

As the company continued to develop space technology, Musk became increasingly aware of the intricacies of space flight. He knew he needed more funding to get his projects launched, so he sought out partners who might help fund his vision. In 2006, NASA became interested in such a partnership. NASA's Commercial Orbital Transportation Services division awarded SpaceX $278 million to be part of a new project. The project invited private companies to develop spacecraft capable of reaching the International Space Station (ISS), a multinational research station orbiting Earth.

Who Is Elon Musk?

Elon Musk, born in South Africa on June 28, 1971, is an American entrepreneur known for his innovations in technology. He showed early talent in computing, selling a video game at age 12. After moving to the U.S. in 1988, he earned degrees in economics and physics from the University of Pennsylvania. He briefly considered Stanford for graduate school but pursued entrepreneurship instead. By 2002, he had founded and sold Zip2 and PayPal, later launching Tesla and SpaceX.

SpaceX was one of two companies selected to participate in the project and receive funding. The other was a company named Rocketplane Kistler. The project included specific technology **milestones** that the companies were expected to achieve, and NASA even provided additional funding as those milestones were met.

Although Rocketplane Kistler was eventually dropped from the program, SpaceX's successes led to an expanded partnership. The company eventually received a total of $396 million from NASA to continue pioneering work in private space travel.

By March 2006, SpaceX had its first Falcon 1 ready for testing. The rocket was designed to ultimately deliver satellites into orbit. During the test, SpaceX simply hoped the rocket would reach orbit, because various setbacks had delayed the test for months. The main setback was related to the fuel used to propel the rocket—the liquid oxygen used as fuel boiled at too high a rate. As a result, the rocket ran out of fuel before it could successfully launch. SpaceX arranged to have extra liquid oxygen on standby for their March launch and developed a plan to cool the oxygen if delays occurred.

As the time approached for the March test, SpaceX and NASA were excited about the prospect of the rocket's success. The total price for the first Falcon 1 rocket came in at $6.7 million—an absolute bargain for NASA, whose typical rockets cost about three times as much. If SpaceX could keep launch prices low, it could greatly benefit space travel.

On March 24, SpaceX readied the first Falcon 1 for liftoff. They followed standard protocols to ensure its success. Although the liftoff was delayed by a little more than an hour, everything seemed ready when the countdown reached zero at 5:30 PM (EST) on Kwajalein Atoll in the Pacific. At that time, the Merlin engines erupted, producing close to 77,000 pounds of thrust—enough to send the 70-foot rocket off the launch pad.

However, shortly after takeoff, pieces began to jettison from the rocket. About 26 seconds after launch, the rocket started moving erratically. Fifteen seconds later, it crashed into the Pacific Ocean.

Subsequent studies found that corrosion had occurred between the fuel line and a nut inside the rocket. This sparked an engine fire that destroyed the rocket. Despite a total loss, SpaceX learned from the experience and prepared for a second test flight. This flight, which had been scheduled before the loss of the first Falcon 1,

The SpaceX rocket explodes mid-flight

was designed to carry a United States Naval Satellite into space.

SpaceX spent nearly a year perfecting the second version of the Falcon 1. The updated version stood about 68 feet tall. Like its predecessor, it was a two-stage rocket designed to deliver a **payload** of slightly more than 1,250 pounds into space. The cost to launch the new Falcon 1 was $7 million, slightly more expensive than the first rocket. The first stage of the rocket was designed to be reusable. It was equipped with a set of parachutes, allowing it to return safely to Earth with the goal of landing in the Pacific Ocean. The second stage would blast off from the first, propelling itself into orbit.

The second trial took place almost one year after the first. Launched again from Kwajalein Atoll, the second launch was met with considerable anticipation. SpaceX

Falcon Test Trials

The Falcon test trials carried some interesting cargo. The first Falcon 1 carried a satellite built by cadets at the U.S. Air Force Academy. The third Falcon 1 test carried perhaps an even more interesting payload: it took two small satellites on board, as well as a satellite known as the Trailblazer. This satellite was designed for the Pentagon. The trial also carried a "burial payload"—the cremated remains of people who wanted to be buried in space. This included the remains of actor James Doohan, who played "Scotty," the chief engineer, on the original Star Trek television series and subsequent movies.

implemented hundreds of improvements to its system, hoping that a year of development would pay off. The goal of the mission was for the rocket to successfully liftoff, reach a distance of 485 miles from Earth, and then begin its return to the planet—ideally within ten minutes of liftoff.

After a short delay, liftoff for the second trial was set for March 20. As the clock hit 9:10 (EDT), the rocket lifted off from the launch pad. As the first stage ended and the second stage began, this trial achieved more than the first test: the rocket entered space. After about five minutes, it reached an altitude of 186 miles from Earth before encountering a problem with its roll control. It reentered the Earth's atmosphere earlier than planned and plunged into the Pacific Ocean.

Although the second trial did not proceed as planned, it accomplished more than the first and was viewed as a success by SpaceX. According to Elon Musk, "We successfully reached space, and really retired almost all of the risk associated with the rocket."

SpaceX scheduled the third test flight more than a year later. As part of the mission plan, engineers redesigned the Merlin engine that powered the Falcon 1. They built the new rocket to run on a mix of kerosene and liquid oxygen, which reduced the burn rate and saved fuel.

This trial was scheduled to lift off from Kwajalein Atoll on August 2, 2008. As with the previous two flights, all seemed normal as the rocket lifted off from the ground. The third trial raced into the sky. At two minutes and twenty seconds after liftoff, the second stage began blasting off from the first. However, the thrust from the newly designed engine caused the first stage to strike the second stage, sending both stages careening into the Pacific Ocean.

Despite the third "failure," SpaceX felt confident about the trial. They had collected data that they knew would help make the fourth trial successful. That is exactly what they did on September 28, 2008.

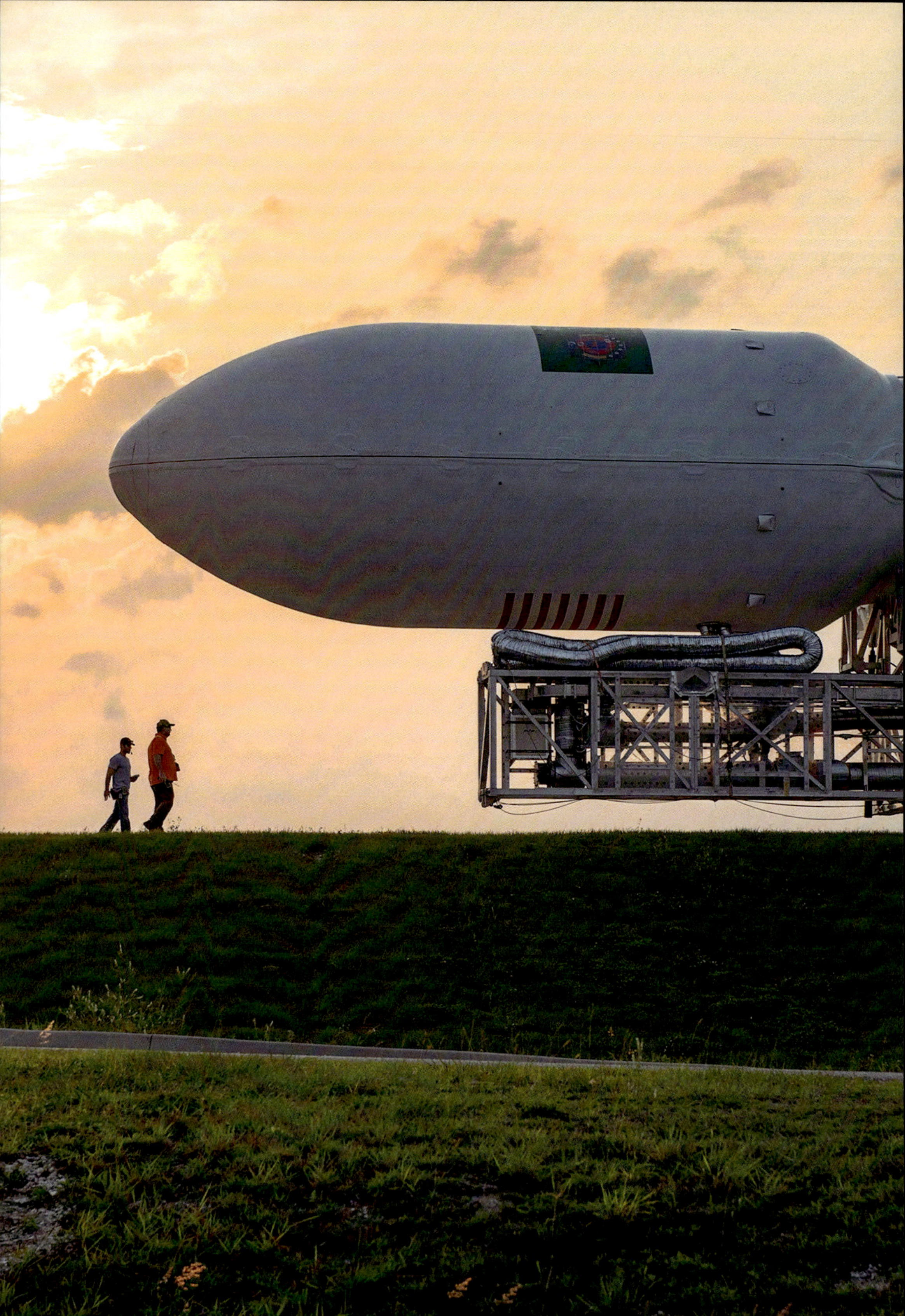

Tackling Space

Following the successful test flight of Falcon 1, SpaceX sent Falcon 1 on one more mission in 2009 before retiring it. The company had already begun working on a new rocket called Falcon 9. Falcon 9 was designed to resemble the original Falcon—it stood at the same height as Falcon 1 and incorporated a reusable orbiter to keep the costs of space travel low.

OPPOSITE: A two-stage rocket used for launching satellites, cargo, and crewed missions. It features a reusable first stage that lands vertically after launch.

It also used the same Merlin engine as the Falcon 1 trials. However this rocket was designed to bring heavier payloads into space. The payload weight varied depending on the destination—whether into orbit or to the ISS—and on the amount of fuel required.

The first test flight of Falcon 9 occurred on June 4, 2010. The rocket included an early version of the Dragon spacecraft that SpaceX had been designing for several years. This spacecraft was the prototype of the

Dragon craft that SpaceX could send either to orbit the Earth or to travel to the ISS.

At 1:30 PM (EDT), Falcon 9 took off from Cape Canaveral, Florida. Although the rocket rolled slightly after liftoff, it successfully launched. During its second stage, it sent the unmanned Dragon prototype into orbit. The Dragon remained in orbit for three weeks before returning to Earth.

What Does the Dragon Take to and from the ISS?

You may wonder what the Dragon carries to and from the ISS besides supplies. Simply put: a lot of interesting experiments. One experiment delivered by the Dragon in 2014 was nicknamed "Veggie." This prototype garden tested how red romaine lettuce grows in space. The test results provided data on how well food can be grown and harvested in space for future missions. The Dragon has also returned with some intriguing cargo, including blood and urine samples from ISS astronauts to study how their bodies cope with extended periods in space.

This initial test flight paved the way for a second test flight on December 8, 2010. That flight included a more complete version of the Dragon spacecraft. The second test was designed to demonstrate to NASA that the Dragon could successfully enter orbit and be used to deliver payloads into space. Following the success of this mission, the partnership between NASA and SpaceX was solidified, paving the way for a third mission on May 22, 2012. During this mission, Falcon 9 successfully launched a Dragon into orbit to deliver cargo to the ISS.

Delivering cargo to the ISS was just the first step in a larger partnership between NASA and SpaceX. NASA contracted with SpaceX to join the Commercial Resupply Services program. As a result, SpaceX agreed to launch 20 resupply missions to the ISS between October 2012 and March 2020. These missions delivered more

than 95,000 pounds (43,000 kg) of cargo to the ISS and returned 76,000 pounds (34,400 kg) of cargo to Earth.

SpaceX continued to improve and modify Falcon 9. Along with these improvements, SpaceX began using its rockets for missions developed by other countries. The company partnered with the Canadian Space Agency to

Starman

In 2018, SpaceX launched a Falcon Heavy rocket carrying Elon Musk's personal Tesla Roadster as a test payload to showcase the rocket's capabilities. Rather than using a conventional dummy mass, Musk chose the car—complete with a mannequin named Starman—to inspire public interest in spaceflight and symbolize future interplanetary travel. The vehicle was placed into an elliptical orbit around the Sun, crossing Mars' orbital path. Since its launch, it has completed multiple solar orbits and made close approaches to Mars and Earth.

carry the Canadian research satellite, CALLIOPE, into space. Launched on September 29, 2013, this satellite was the first small satellite created by the Canadian agency. It was used to study the upper part of Earth's atmosphere, known as the **ionosphere**, as well as space storms.

As SpaceX continued to refine its Falcon 9 rockets, its engineers also turned their attention to the Dragon spacecraft. In 2014, NASA approached SpaceX about manned missions using the Dragon. The company soon unveiled its reimagined version of the Dragon spacecraft that could carry astronauts. This new craft was designed to carry seven astronauts into space. It included life support systems not present on previous versions, an emergency escape system, and state-of-the-art equipment for piloting the ship. The manned version also featured improvements to the ISS **docking system**. Whereas the

> “SPACEX CONTINUED TO IMPROVE AND MODIFY FALCON 9.”

unmanned Dragon was secured to the ISS by a large robotic arm, the manned Dragon docked directly with the station.

After five years of work on the Dragon, SpaceX launched the first test flight of the updated spacecraft on March 2, 2019. A Falcon 9 carried the spacecraft—which included an **anthropomorphic test dummy** named Ripley, outfitted with various instruments to record data that might affect live astronauts—into space. The test mission successfully docked with the ISS on March 3 and remained in orbit for several days before returning to Earth on March 8.

Other SpaceX Endeavors

In 2014, SpaceX devised a plan to bring Internet service to remote parts of the world. As part of that plan, they wanted to create an Internet constellation of satellites called WorldVu. WorldVu would not be a constellation of stars. Rather, this constellation refers to a network of satellites in the atmosphere that provide internet access to people throughout the world.

OPPOSITE: A SpaceX rocket leaves a trail across the atmosphere

How to See Starlink

Over the past decade, spotting Starlink satellites has become a popular pastime for amateur astronomers and space enthusiasts. Seen as a string of evenly spaced lights moving across the night sky, they're often mistaken for "alien spacecraft." Several tracking apps make viewing easier—Find Starlink, for example, lets users enter their location to see when and where the satellites will be visible.

The actual WorldVu project never fully got off the ground. Yet, in January 2015, SpaceX announced the creation of a similar program called Starlink. The United States gave the company permission to launch 4,000 satellites into what is called **low Earth orbit**—a region of the Earth's atmosphere within about 1,200 miles of the surface, where objects like the ISS orbit. At the time, Musk explained, "We're really talking about something which is, in the long term, like rebuilding the Internet in space." However, he was only just starting to scratch the surface of the plan and later expanded that vision to include 10,000 satellites or more.

The following year, SpaceX applied for a permit from the **Federal Communications Commission** (FCC) to launch more than 4,000 satellites as part of this eventual Internet constellation. Two years later, in February 2018, the first two test satellites were launched. Called Tintin A and Tintin B, these satellites provided valuable data for SpaceX to start developing a working constellation system. However, the data also suggested that the satellites should be placed in a lower orbit. In May 2019, the first official launch deployed 60 satellites aboard a Falcon 9. They were placed in a lower orbit with permission from the FCC, and SpaceX opened access to the satellites for public use in November 2020.

Since then, more than 6,000 satellites have been launched as part of the Starlink system, and more than three million people have subscribed to the service. These subscribers use small satellite dishes to access the Internet.

The success of Starlink has led SpaceX to expand its vision into other fields. They have developed a prototype military satellite constellation system for the U.S. military

SPACEX

called Starshield, and they have also created plans to partner with at least one mobile phone company to provide mobile service. As a bonus, people can watch the satellites pass overhead—resembling a string of bright, white lights racing across the sky. They look like a pearl necklace trailing across the heavens and are considered quite a spectacle to those who catch a glimpse.

Despite its successes, Starlink is not without controversy. The **International Astronomical Union** has criticized the constellation, arguing that the large number of satellites poses a threat to the launch of future satellites. They also believe the satellites pose a danger to other objects in space. Similar concerns were raised by the Chinese government in 2021. According to a report they submitted to the United Nations, China's Tianhe space station had to maneuver twice to avoid colliding with the satellite network.

Other astronomical groups have been critical of Starlink for its potential impact on space observations. The American Astronomical Society voiced concern that constellations like Starlink add unnecessary light pollution to the sky—making the night sky brighter and hindering the study of faint objects in space. The society also suggested that having too many constellations could even brighten the daytime sky, as sunlight reflects off the satellites and increases overall atmospheric brightness.

After studying the issue, SpaceX determined that the sunlight often reflects off these satellites in directions other than toward the ground. Nonetheless, SpaceX has taken measures to alleviate the possibility of excessive brightening. Initially, they began coating newer satellites with a type of paint designed to darken them. However, those measures did not fully control the reflection. Consequently, Starlink developed a visor-like solution called VisorSat. Small "visors" are placed on satellites prior to launch, working like a sun visor or umbrella to block

What Is the Artemis Project?

The **Artemis Project**—sometimes called the Artemis Program—is NASA's official program to return humans to the Moon. It is named after the Greek goddess of the Moon, Artemis. The program comprises four missions, nicknamed Artemis I through Artemis IV. Artemis I involved an unmanned voyage around the Moon. The second mission will include the first manned test flight of the Orion spacecraft around the Moon. The third mission will involve sending humans to the Moon's South Pole to locate potential sites for a future lunar base, and the final mission will include the development of a space station called Gateway that will orbit the Moon.

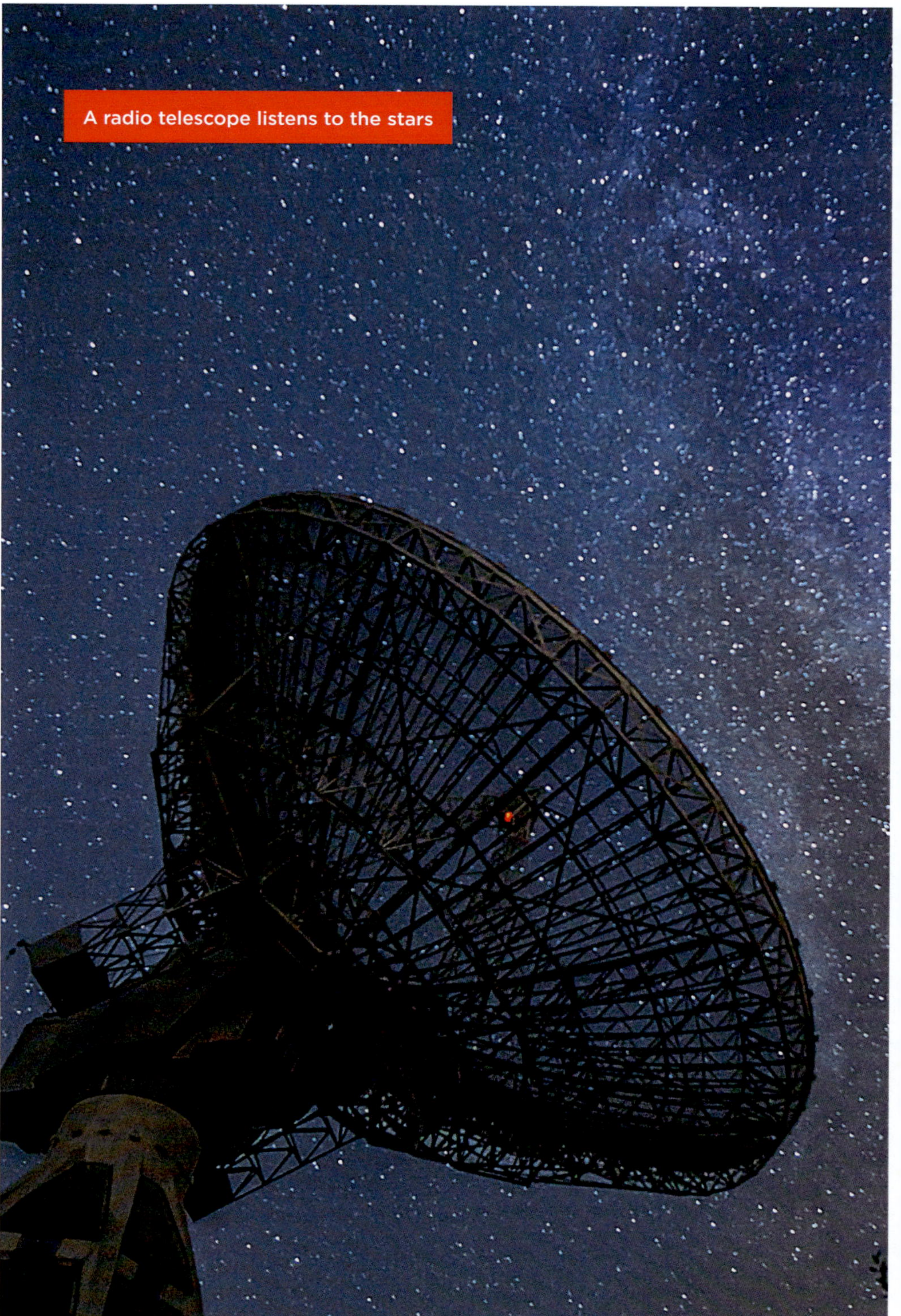

A radio telescope listens to the stars

sunlight from reflecting off the white surfaces, thereby reducing brightness.

The impact of such constellations is also a concern for those who study space using **radio telescopes**. These telescopes examine radio signals from space, including signals emitted by elements such as hydrogen—which forms stars and other celestial objects—and are used in the search for **extraterrestrial life.** However, radio telescopes must share frequencies with satellites. As more satellites and constellations like Starlink launch, competition for these radio signals increases.

As NASA's plans to explore the Moon and Mars continue to unfold, the agency has further partnered with SpaceX to develop the technology required to reach these distant destinations. As part of this partnership, SpaceX has embarked on several coordinated projects.

For the first phase, SpaceX began working on different projects connected to these missions. One project involved creating a reusable spacecraft that could carry larger payloads into space—this led to the development of the Starship, a reusable craft designed to operate in low Earth orbit and beyond.

SpaceX developed two distinct configurations of this craft. One configuration is designed to carry massive payloads—potentially even larger than the James Webb Space Telescope—into space. The other is designed to carry humans; this version of Starship is planned to carry up to 100 astronauts into orbit or beyond.

Another phase of the project involved creating a new super rocket capable of carrying a payload of more than 220,000 pounds (100,000 kg) into space. This rocket, dubbed Super Heavy (not "Space Heavy"), is the most powerful rocket ever assembled. It is a reusable booster designed to carry Starship into low Earth orbit. Together, Super Heavy and Starship stand 394 feet (120 meters) tall, making them the first reusable rocket and spacecraft system of their kind.

Although Super Heavy and Starship are still under development, SpaceX has already plans for their use. The ultimate goal of Starship is to transport astronauts to the lunar surface as part of the Artemis III and Artemis IV missions. In the future, Musk envisions that

OPPOSITE Starship ignition test in 2024.

Starship will also help transport astronauts to Mars as part of later missions.

Starship will eventually be able to launch from both the NASA site at Cape Canaveral and the SpaceX site in Boca Chica, Texas. The first test flights began at Boca Chica in 2019, using a prototype called Starhopper to test the spacecraft's control systems. A year later, SpaceX began testing the first full-sized prototypes of Starship. The initial four test flights resulted in failures, with multiple prototypes exploding during trials. How-

“IN 2020, SPACEX BEGAN TESTING THE FIRST FULL-SIZED PROTOTYPES OF STARSHIP”

ever, in March 2021, the first successful Starship trial occurred—it was able to liftoff and fly at an altitude of six miles above Earth before returning safely.

Testing has continued into current times. On January 16, 2025, a new prototype called Starship Upper Stage 2 was tested. This craft, attached to a Super Heavy booster, was launched from Boca Chica. The new Starship included modifications over previous versions and could launch satellites. It was also slightly larger than earlier models. However, when launched with a Super Heavy booster from Texas on that day, the spacecraft

experienced a problem during the second stage and ultimately exploded. The Super Heavy booster, however, returned safely to Earth and was recovered. This test was the first of at least twelve planned Starship tests for the year, paving the way for what SpaceX hopes will soon lead to routine space travel.

NASA
NASA
NASA

The Future of SpaceX

While SpaceX currently serves as a vital private partner for government space missions, the company remains keenly focused on the future. There are several missions that SpaceX hopes to be a part of in the coming decades.

OPPOSITE: SpaceX CEO and Chief Designer Elon Musk, left, NASA astronauts Victor Glover, Doug Hurley, Bob Behnken, NASA Administrator Jim Bridenstine, and NASA astronaut Mike Hopkins.

SpaceX is currently working on a spacecraft that can help NASA's Artemis Project return people to the Moon for the first time since 1972. As part of this project, SpaceX is developing a version of the Starship called the Starship Human Landing System (also known as the Starship HLS).

The goal of the Starship HLS is to transport astronauts to and from the surface of the Moon. To reach the Moon, the HLS would first enter lunar orbit. Using one of its multiple docking systems, the HLS would dock with a small space station called Gateway—a proposed platform that will orbit the Moon and house astronauts. Astronauts would transfer from Gateway into the HLS while it is docked, and then the HLS would transport them to the Moon. Once on the lunar surface, they could explore, conduct studies, and gather samples of rock and

View from the International space station

NASA
ARTEMIS

OPPOSITE An artist's rendering of the HLS Moon lander.

soil. The HLS would then bring the astronauts and collected samples back to Gateway, and eventually return them to Earth.

The HLS is one of several proposed lunar landers currently in development. NASA hopes to have multiple companies produce these landers to reduce costs while enabling several missions to the Moon, possibly simultaneously. Like all proposed landers, the HLS must be versatile—it must handle the rugged and varied terrain of the Moon and include life support systems that allow astronauts to remain onboard while they explore.

Central to the HLS mission is NASA's plan to transport astronauts to the Moon on a regular basis. This will eventually pave the way for the exploration and settlement of the Moon's South Pole, where astronauts could establish a Moon base, develop new space technologies, and use the colony as a training ground for future missions to Mars.

Another mission SpaceX is developing is a towing system for the International Space Station (ISS). The ISS is one of the space stations currently orbiting Earth. Although it has been inhabited by astronauts since 2000, it became fully operational nine years later. The ISS has served as the home to astronauts from twenty different countries and has exemplified international scientific goodwill. For the past twenty years, there has been at least one human aboard the ISS as astronauts come and go.

However, like earlier space stations such as MIR or Skylab, the ISS has a limited lifespan. According to Russian sources, nearly 80 percent of the parts of the ISS that they helped build are at or past their design

“ANOTHER MISSION SPACEX IS DEVELOPING IS A TOWING SYSTEM FOR THE INTERNATIONAL SPACE STATION (ISS).”

life. Reports suggest that the cargo module is beginning to show signs of age and is developing cracks.

As a result, Russia has committed to helping maintain the ISS until 2028, while the remaining partner countries have agreed to operate the ISS until 2030, when it will be permanently decommissioned. However, this raises a new question: what will happen to the ISS once it is no longer in use?

OPPOSITE NASA astronauts wearing SpaceX spacesuits.

Unfortunately, officials cannot simply leave the ISS in orbit. Without astronauts to man it and to steer it away from space debris, the ISS could be struck by objects in orbit, resulting in a deluge of space debris. Additionally, if left unattended, the ISS loses about 328 feet (or 100 meters) of altitude each day due to drag from Earth's residual atmosphere. Astronauts periodically boost the ISS to maintain a safe orbit; without this reboost, the ISS would eventually plummet to Earth, potentially disintegrating over populated areas.

This is where SpaceX comes in. NASA awarded $1 billion to SpaceX to develop a towing system to bring the ISS back to Earth. This system would consist of a SpaceX Dragon craft that would attach to the ISS once it reaches a predetermined point in orbit. The Dragon would then tug the ISS into the atmosphere for a **controlled reentry**.

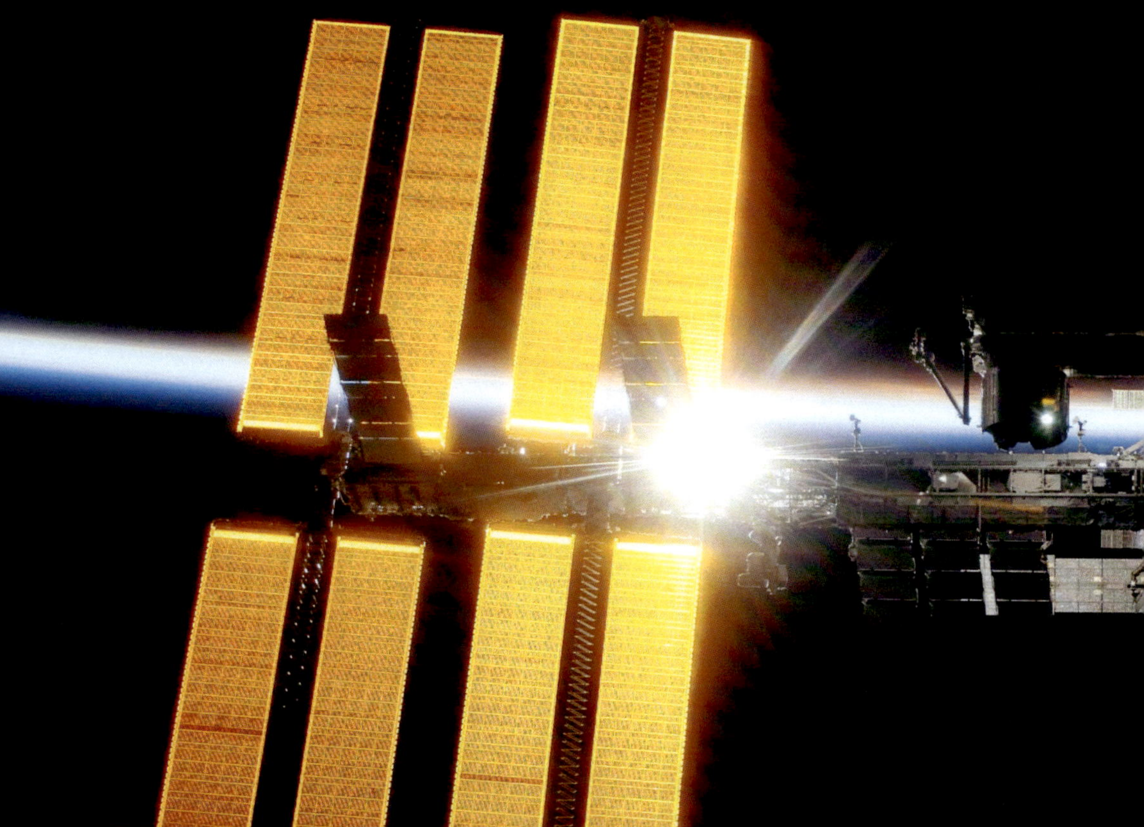

What Is the ISS?

Although the ISS has been in orbit since 2000, work on the space station began in 1984, when the U.S. Congress appropriated funds for its development. Between 1984 and 1993, scientists from the United States, Europe, Canada, and Japan worked on designing the space station. In 1993, members of the Russian space agency joined the project, and in 1998 they began launching elements to assemble the station. Since then, space agencies from these five regions have continued to operate the ISS, which has been home to more than 270 astronauts.

This means SpaceX would have some control over where the ISS ultimately reenters, targeting a desolate part of the Pacific Ocean known as Point Nemo. The heat of reentry would burn off or break up smaller parts of the ISS, starting with the solar panels. The one-hour descent would cause the ISS to resemble a giant meteor, and eventually, most of the ISS would disintegrate in the atmosphere—with any remnants hopefully landing on the ocean floor.

Perhaps the greatest long-term goal of SpaceX is to initiate human spaceflight to Mars within the coming decade. Mars has long been a target for human habitation by various space agencies. Although Mars is a dry, sandy planet, it contains frozen water sources and offers potential for future colonization.

SpaceX is currently developing plans to send a series of five unmanned missions to Mars, starting in 2026. These missions will help SpaceX learn about the challenges involved in human travel to Mars, including how to land on and take off from the planet. If the test missions are successful, the first crewed mission to Mars could occur two years after the initial test.

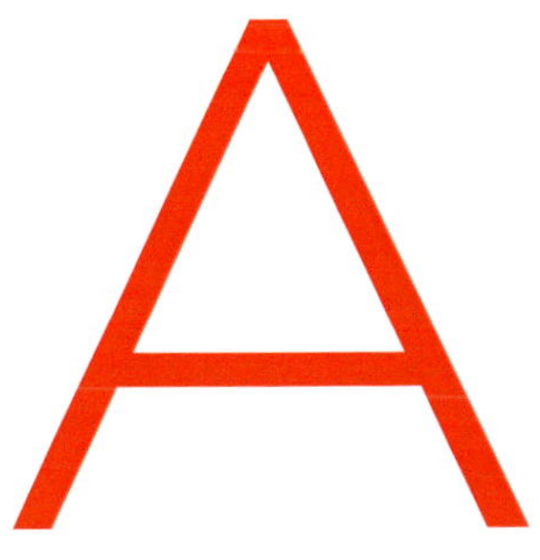

lthough NASA and other space agencies have expressed interest in sending humans to Mars, Musk hopes to speed up the process. He envisions that this will eventually lead to the development of a space colony on Mars. His company is modifying its plans for the Starships that would travel there. These vehicles could be large enough to accommodate amenities such as a movie theater and a running track to help colonizers stay fit, while also providing entertainment.

SpaceX has even begun developing plans for a domed city on Mars. This city would consist of smaller domes arranged in circles around a larger central dome, all interconnected. In time, plants, animals, and astronauts would be transported to the Red Planet. The plans also include sending solar panels to power the colony and investigating ways to warm the planet, including ice harvesting. While the plan is ambitious, SpaceX envisions establishing the first Martian colony sometime in the 2040s.

SpaceX – To Infinity and Beyond

Although SpaceX plans to visit Mars in the next decade, Elon Musk has suggested that his ambitions extend even further. He envisions that future versions of Starship will be capable of traveling beyond Mars. Musk has often stated that the future of the human race involves exploring the stars, and he has proposed that future SpaceX Starships might eventually carry humans beyond our solar system—to distant star systems at some point in the future.

Selected Bibliography

Dobrijevic, Daisy . "Starlink Satellite Train: How to See and Track It in the Night Sky." Space.com, 21 Apr. 2023, www.space.com/starlink-satellite-train-how-to-see-and-track-it.

Evans, Ben. "Ten Years of History-Making: The Remarkable Decade of the Falcon 9." AmericaSpace, 5 June 2020, www.americaspace.com/2020/06/05/ten-years-of-history-making-the-remarkable-decade-of-the-falcon-9/.

Hart, Robert. "Elon Musk Says Future SpaceX Starship "Will Travel to Other Star Systems" after Rocket's Latest Test." *Forbes*, 18 Mar. 2024, www.forbes.com/sites/roberthart/2024/03/18/elon-musk-says-future-spacex-starship-will-travel-to-other-star-systems-after-rockets-latest-test/.

Howell, Elizabeth. "Astronauts to Grow Lettuce in Space with NASA Veggie Farm." Space.com, Space, 13 Apr. 2014, www.space.com/25478-astronauts-space-lettuce-nasa-veggie-farm.html.

"Human Landing Systems - NASA." NASA, www.nasa.gov/reference/human-landing-systems/.

"NASA's Artemis IV: Building First Lunar Space Station - NASA." NASA, 29 Mar. 2024, www.nasa.gov/general/nasas-artemis-iv-building-first-lunar-space-station/.

Pultarova, Tereza, and Elizabeth Howell. "Starlink: SpaceX's Satellite Internet Project." Space.com, 1 July 2024, www.space.com/spacex-starlink-satellites.html.

Ray, Justin. "Spaceflight Now | Falcon Launch Report | First SpaceX Rocket Launch Ends in Failure." Spaceflightnow.com, 2025, spaceflightnow.com/falcon/f1/060324failure.html. Accessed 15 Jan. 2025.

Reuters. "SpaceX Plans to Send Five Uncrewed Starships to Mars in Two Years, Musk Says." *Reuters*, 22 Sept. 2024, www.reuters.com/science/musk-says-spacex-plans-launch-about-five-uncrewed-starships-mars-two-years-2024-09-22/.

September 2008, Tariq Malik 29. "SpaceX Successfully Launches Falcon 1 Rocket into Orbit." Space.com, www.space.com/5905-spacex-successfully-launches-falcon-1-rocket-orbit.html.

Glossary

Artemis Project a NASA project designed to return spacecraft and humans to the moon and eventually establish a colony there

anthropomorphic test dummy a mannequin device sent into space in place of humans, often with tools to conduct measurements of the effects of space on humans

controlled reentry a process by which a spacecraft is maneuvered by operators to ensure re-enters the Earth's atmosphere in a specific region to minimize the damage it could cause to populated areas

docking system a system that allows one object to dock and berth with another one in space

extraterrestrial life life from a world other than Earth

Federal Communications Commission (FCC) an independent agency of the United States that regulates cable, radio, satellite, television, and wire communications

International Astronomical Union
an international organization that helps to promote and safeguard all aspects of astronomy

ionosphere the region of the upper Earth atmosphere extending from 30 miles (50 km) to 370 miles (600 km) above the surface of the planet

low Earth orbit the region of the Earth's atmosphere within 1,200 miles of the Earth's surface where objects like the ISS are in orbit

milestones certain markers in a project that are expected to be met by certain periods of time

NASA the official United States space agency which coordinates space research and space travel for the country

payload the load carried by a spacecraft (or other vehicle) excluding the actual craft itself

radio telescopes a special type of radio receiver and antenna used to detect radio waves emitted from astronomical objects

space race the term used to describe the space competition between the United States and the Soviet Union from 1957 with the launch of the Sputnik satellite until 1969 with the American landing on the moon

Websites

NASA

https://www.nasa.gov/

This is the official website of the National Aeronautics and Space administration. It provides up to the minute information about space launches, space discoveries, and current events related to space.

Space X

https://www.spacex.com/

This is the official site of the Space X corporation. It provides details on the history, missions, and projects developed by Space X.

Site: Find Star Link

https://findstarlink.com/

This website helps track Star Link and helps viewers determine when Starlink will be detected in their nighttime sky.

Index